People in the Community

Police
Officers

Diyan Leake

Heinemann Library
Chicago, Illinois

Customer Service 888-454-2279
Visit our website at www.heinemannraintree.com

Designed by Joanna Hinton-Malivoire and Steve Mead
Printed in China by Leo Paper Group

12 11 10
10 9 8 7 6 5 4 3 2

Library of Congress Cataloguing-in-Publication Data
Leake, Diyan.
   Police officers / Diyan Leake.
      p. cm. -- (People in the community)
   Includes bibliographical references and index.
   ISBN 978-1-4329-1190-4 (hc) -- ISBN 978-1-4329-1197-3 (pb) 1. Police--Juvenile literature. 2. Police-community relations--Juvenile literature. I. Title.
   HV7922.L43 2008
   363.2--dc22
                              2007045068

Acknowledgments
The publishers would like to thank the following for permission to reproduce photographs:
©Age Fotostock pp. **6** (UpperCut Images), **8** (Jeremy Woodhouse), **11** (Anton J. Geisser), **12** (Kevin O'Hara), **14** (Ben Walsh), **16** (Gonzalo Azumendi), **21** (Jeff Greenberg), **22 (bottom)** (Kevin O'Hara); ©Alamy pp. **9** (Vehbi Koca), **15** (Mike Abrahams), **22 (middle)** (Mike Abrahams); ©AP Photo (Remy de la Mauviniere) p. **19**; ©Corbis (Bojan Brecelj) p. **13**; ©DigitalRailroad.net (GalileoPix/Oote Boe) p. **7**; ©Getty Images pp. **4** (Gavin Hellier), **5** (Andrew Holt), **10** (Jeff Brass), **20** (Yoshikazu Tsuno/AFP), **22 (top)** (Gavin Hellier); ©Reuters (Rafiqur Rahman/Landov) p. **18**; ©Shutterstock (Pres Panayotov) p. **17**.

Front cover photograph of a police officer on horseback reproduced with permission of ©Reuters (Ian Hodgson). Back cover photograph reproduced with permission of ©Age Fotostock (Jeremy Woodhouse).

Every effort has been made to contact copyright holders of any material reproduced in this book. Any omissions will be rectified in subsequent printings if notice is given to the publisher.

Contents

Communities

People live in communities.

People work in communities.

Police Officers in the Community

Police officers work in communities.

Police officers help people stay safe.

What Police Officers Do

Police officers help keep traffic safe.

Police officers help people who
are lost.

Police officers help with accidents.

Police officers help fight crime.

What Police Officers Wear

Police officers wear uniforms.

Police officers wear badges.

Where Police Officers Work

Police officers work on the streets.

Police officers work in police stations.

Police Officers on the Go

Police officers drive cars.

Police officers walk.

Police officers ride horses.

Police officers ride bikes.

How Police Officers Help Us

Police officers help people stay safe.

Police officers help the community.

Picture Glossary

community group of people living and working in the same area

police station building where police officers work

uniform special clothes that a certain group of people wear

Index

Note to Parents and Teachers

This series introduces readers to the lives of different community workers, and explains some of the different jobs they perform around the world. Some of the locations featured in this book include Transylvania, Romania (page 4); London, England (page 5); Basel, Switzerland (page 11); Saskatchewan Province, Canada (page 12); Iquitos, Peru (page 16); Vincennes, France (page 19); and Tokyo, Japan (page 20).

Discuss with children their experiences with police officers in the community. Do they know any police officers? Discuss with children why communities need police officers.

Ask children to look through the book and name some of the tools police officers use to help them with their job. Give children poster boards and ask them to draw police officers. Tell them to show the clothes, tools, and vehicles they use to do their job.

The text has been chosen with the advice of a literacy expert to enable beginning readers success while reading independently or with moderate support. You can support children's nonfiction literacy skills by helping them use the table of contents, picture glossary, and index.